LONDON

London Zoo in Regent's Park features a popular children's corner, where the young of several species mingle freely.

LONDON

Swingers and Squares

by YUMIKO KIYOMIYA

 KODANSHA INTERNATIONAL LTD.
TOKYO & NEW YORK

Distributors:

UNITED STATES: *Harper & Row, Publishers, Inc.*
10 East 53rd Street, New York, New York 10022

CANADA: *Fitzhenry & Whiteside Limited*
150 Lesmill Road, Don Mills, Ontario

CENTRAL AND SOUTH AMERICA: *Feffer & Simons Inc.*
31 Union Square, New York, New York 10003

EUROPE: *Boxerbooks Inc.*
Limmatstrasse 111, 8031 Zurich

THAILAND: *Central Department Store Ltd.*
306 Silom Road, Bangkok

HONG KONG: *Books for Asia Ltd.*
379 Prince Edward Road, Kowloon

THE FAR EAST: *Japan Publications Trading Company*
P.O. Box 5030, Tokyo International, Tokyo

Published by Kodansha International Ltd., 2-12-21 Otowa, Bunkyo-ku,
Tokyo 112, and Kodansha International/USA, Ltd., 10 East 53rd
Street, New York, New York 10022. Copyright © 1973 by Kodansha
International Ltd.

LCC 72-96126
ISBN 0-87011-198-1
JBC 0026-783888-2361

First edition, 1973

Contents

Drawings by Hirobumi Nagakane

Swingers and Squares

After some five years of doing commercial photography for slick Japanese magazines, I came to the sad conclusion that I had by then spent half of my unrecoverable twenties accomplishing nothing that I truly wanted to do. To earn my living during those years I had photographed what the magazines I worked for ordered, mainly the famous or notorious of the world: popular singers, well-known actors, convicted criminals, presidents of large corporations, even members of the imperial family; or else I had been constrained to exercise what photographic talent I possessed on a package of instant noodles, an expensively dressed fashion model, or a professionally decorated room. Only gradually, as my disinterest in all the work I was doing increased, did I realize that what I yearned to photograph was the ordinary folk of the world, folk whose faces were not rigid public masks, as in a No play, but rather reflections of an inner identity.

Accordingly, I decided to become a free lance, accepting commercial assignments when I had to but for the most part wandering through the streets of Tokyo, where plain people lived, taking their pictures as I could. I even invaded the few slum areas that still exist in our modern, prosperous capital (an invasion, incidentally, that

LONDON

called for a bit of courage on the part of a young woman alone), for it seemed to me that it was in the poor and the outcast of the world that I was to find what I was looking for. The results of these labors were shown in an exhibit called "Slum Street Reportage."

Although the exhibit itself was rather a success, I experienced as I wandered through it a deep sense of dissatisfaction. Had I not, I asked myself, depended too greatly for my effects on the poverty and squalor of the slums and their denizens? Could not anyone with a good camera have taken the same pictures? Were the masks of failure truly very different from the masks of success?

I then determined to see if I could not express what I wanted in photographs of children before the masks had had a chance to form—children growing up in dissimilar environments and showing the differing effects of those environments. This exhibit, called "Children Are Difficult Beings," was less successful than the earlier one, from the public's point of view as well as from my own, and I felt myself plunged into despair. It seemed to me that the Japanese at that time (the year was 1965) were obsessed by eccentric and grotesque photography and were quite uninterested in the kind of pictures I had wanted to take—pictures that the simplest, least sophisticated grandmother in the remotest village could understand and appreciate.

My deep dissatisfaction with this exhibition persuaded me to abandon entirely all thought of photography as a means of self-expression. From then on it was to provide no more than my bowl of rice or my bread and butter, and I accepted the barest minimum of commissions—only enough to supply me with life's daily requirements. Aside from that, I did almost nothing. I simply stayed home; I, who had always been so active, was now sunk in lethargy. I fell back upon my own emptiness. When I could bring myself to read at all, I read the gloomiest, most melancholy books which I could find.

It was in this state of feeling that I was suffering from "the sickness unto death" (to steal a phrase from Kierkegaard) that I received a visit from a reporter friend who had come to say farewell. He was on his way to London, to begin a long assignment there. Shocked by my pale, hollow-eyed face, he insisted that what I needed was a total change of scene—and that London was the ideal place to provide it. I had been to Europe before and felt no great enthusiasm for the project, but he spoke on, and after he left I thought a great deal about what he had said and suddenly came to the conclusion that he was right. I would go to London, and I would stay there for at least two years. I would, of course, accept commercial assignments, having no choice in the matter, but my chief effort would be devoted to learning to know the city and its people. Then I would be able to photograph what I had come to know, although I was far from feeling either so sanguine or so presumptuous as to suppose myself capable of producing a photographic masterpiece exposing the inner life of the people of a foreign city.

That decision of mine had several consequences: I spent two and a half years in London; I came to love it and its people; back in Japan I had two shows of my London pictures (some of which satisfied even me!); and—perhaps most important of all—I felt myself cured of that "sickness unto death." We Japanese do not go in much for naming sins, but I knew that I had been wantonly indulging in that deadly one called by Christians "sloth." London delivered me from it; is it surprising that I should feel a debt of gratitude to

9

that great city? One of the purposes of this little book is to help repay my deeply felt sense of obligation.

I left for London the following July (the year was 1968), fortunate in having secured a few commissions that would help keep a roof over my head—for London, so I had been warned, was just as expensive as Tokyo, perhaps for the foreigner unused to English ways even more so. Known as a photographer of children, I was given an assignment to photograph the children of the West; a man's magazine wanted pictures of the "mod" young men of London; and I was also commissioned to do some work for a woman's magazine. All in all, it sounded like enough to keep me both active and in sufficient funds.

After a few days in France, I took the ferry to Dover. Happily, it was a hot, clear July day. All July days in England, I was soon to learn, are not hot and clear, but I was fortunate in my introduction. I was fortunate also in being taken in hand, when the boat docked, by a kindly elderly porter, who saw me standing quite at a loss on deck, surrounded by two large pieces of luggage and my photographic equipment. "I'll look after this," he said, "and meet you in the customs house." And there he was, smiling and waiting. The customs officer, smiling too, did not even ask me to open my bags, and my porter soon installed me on the London train. Tipping being relatively rare in Japan, I was unsure how much to offer this kind man, so I simply asked him. Although the amount he suggested seemed to me very modest, I felt too unsure of myself to offer more.

My reporter friend had found and taken a small flat for me before my arrival. Unfortunately, he was away on an assignment and so was unable to meet me, but I had no trouble getting a taxi at Victoria

Station. The ride seemed to last forever, although in fact it was only about forty minutes, which is no more remarkable in London than it is in Tokyo.

I had told my friend that I wanted to spend as little on rent as possible, but I had not, I must confess, anticipated that the neighborhood would be quite so gloomy. It was a district of old, formerly middle class houses in North London and seemed almost intolerably dismal as we drove up a short hill toward the house where I was to live. By then night was drawing in, the imitation gas lamps that illuminated the street had been turned on, and as I got out of the cab the face of the driver appeared garish and pale and rather frightening. It seemed to me at that moment very unlikely that I would survive London, let alone be cured by it.

My so-called flat was, in fact, a "bed-sitter," just large enough to contain the essential pieces of furniture, with a tiny kitchen. Although it was not much more inviting than the neighborhood around it, it was redeemed by a spectacular view of London from the east window. Accustomed to the exorbitant rents of Tokyo, I did not find it very expensive—around the equivalent of fifteen dollars a week. Of course there was, as I was soon to discover, the peculiarly English system of buying your gas and electricity as you needed it by inserting coins in a meter.

Until I trained myself always to keep a good supply of coins on hand, sometimes after dozing off I woke up in the evening with no light to read by. However, when later on I compared my experiences with those of a Japanese friend who had taken a room with a London family, I decided the meter system was a good one. My friend's landlady was always after her not to use too much electricity and not to take too many baths, because the utilities were included in her rent, while I could be as extravagant as I liked with my own money, and no one complained. Like most Japanese, I am an obsessive bath taker, but even so, and even in the coldest days of winter, I seldom spent more than five pounds a month for both gas and electricity. Water, happily, was free of charge.

The neighborhood was not, in fact, as inconvenient as I had at first feared: from Piccadilly Circus, for example, the house where I lived was only a twenty-minute subway ride and then a five-minute bus ride. Nor, as I later came to know the city better, did the neighborhood seem any gloomier than other noncentral districts I could have afforded. It would, of course, have been very pleasant to live in a handsome old square in Belgravia, but I knew that was quite beyond me, so for the next two and a half years I stayed up there in the north of London, on a street appropriately named Mountain View Road.

Once I was installed, I set out to investigate the food shops in the neighborhood, for I certainly did not want to eat in restaurants all the time, nor could I afford to—save in the very cheapest ones, where I found the food rather unpleasant on the whole. I discovered I could get almost everything I wanted at local shops, but later, when I came to know the city better, I would indulge in occasional splurges in big department stores, where the food was of the finest quality but rather more expensive than in the neighborhood shops. My chief complaint was the fact that most food shops closed at five or five-thirty in the afternoon—and I never seemed able to organize my life properly, being by nature a spur-of-the-moment shopper.

Not far from where I lived was a laundromat, an institution that is familiar enough in the West but is practically unknown in Japan, where almost every household possesses its own washing machine. At first I used to take my clothes and bed linen to be washed and sit quietly waiting until the job was done, but later, after I became a little more fluent in English, I would gossip with the other women— and eventually found the atmosphere to be rather like that of a public bath in Japan. Total strangers suddenly find themselves exchanging intimate gossip. In time I grew to enjoy enormously my evenings at the local laundromat (which happily remained open until eleven o'clock at night).

Next I set about learning how to find my way around the city. The subway (or the underground or the tube, as I eventually learned to call it) was easy, with its clearly marked signs and different colors for different lines; but I had considerably more difficulty with the familiar red double-decker buses. As my ability to read English improved, I bought a map showing the various bus routes, and then I had no more trouble in that direction.

Where the real trouble came was in myself. From the very beginning I had been of two minds about this journey, and now— after the initial euphoria of arrival—my early misgivings returned in full force, deepened by a kind of self-disgust at my inability to enjoy the excitement of London. There is a Japanese proverb to the effect that a woman's heart is as variable as autumn weather, but I think no woman's heart could possibly be as variable as the climate of London in any season. That first summer came to an abrupt end, autumn was for the most part cold and overcast, and winter seemed to set in early. I soon found that I was increasingly using the rain and the snow as excuses just to stay home and sit by the window. I was doing nothing about the assignments I had undertaken, nor was I learning to know the city. I marveled at the vitality of other

13

LONDON

Japanese visitors who spent the entire day and much of the night in sightseeing; I marveled at it, but I could not share it.

Sitting day after day alone in my room, doing nothing, I became obsessed by the fear that I was going mad—that, at the very least, I was in for some sort of nervous breakdown. If so, was there nothing I could do to prevent it? I feared there was not. In fact, it appeared to me that I was worse off than ever before: unable to help myself, I knew no one who could help me. I could not even talk to the people around me. My great adventure had turned into a disastrous failure.

Then one day, leafing idly through a book of quotations, I happened upon that famous statement of the irascible Doctor Johnson. "Sir," he had said, "when a man is tired of London, he is tired of life; for there is in London all that life can afford." Of course the great doctor, when he spoke those words, had not been thinking about a neurotic little Japanese photographer, but it seemed to me that I could hear his testy voice telling me that a person of my age who pretends to be tired of life had better stop pretending—or else give up entirely. And suddenly I realized that I did not want to give up; one of the most sensible men who ever lived had brought me down to earth again. I had my assignments to do, and although they did not excite me unduly, I also had a great city to learn to know, and, hopefully, its people to photograph.

I now for the first time felt capable of action once again. Obviously enough, before I could do anything else, I needed to learn to speak English. Although I had studied it at my Tokyo high school, I was quite incapable of carrying on a conversation. I now enrolled in a government-sponsored night school which offered classes four evenings a week especially for foreigners. In view of that fact, I was both surprised and disappointed that the major emphasis was not on conversation but rather on grammar. I was taught the uses of the subjunctive, for example, but these I had learned long ago in my high school. What I wanted to learn was how to talk to the people I met, and there my progress was far from startling.

One great compensation was my fellow students—young men and women, mostly from the Continent, who worked during the day and who wanted to improve their English so that they could get better jobs. When school was over for the evening, a group of us used to adjourn to a nearby pub. We must have startled the regular patrons as we gabbled on in our motley accents, speaking broken English tinged with French and German and Greek and Polish and many other languages. But we were determined, and although each of us, no doubt, acquired a bit of everyone else's linguistic idiosyncrasies, we did eventually find ourselves improving. One girl landed a job as stewardess with an airline; another was promoted from maid to receptionist at the hotel where she was working; as for myself, I was at last truly embarked on my love affair with London.

It was my night-school friends who had introduced me to the pub life of London, and I was soon enthralled by it, perhaps because it was my first real taste of English life, perhaps because I sensed at once that the pub was peculiarly and unalterably British. It is wholly unlike anything I have ever encountered anywhere else in the world, and once having tasted its pleasures I would take every opportunity that was offered to explore new pubs as I wandered about the city.

Of course the word itself meant nothing to me, but one of my school friends explained it was short for "public house," which in turn was a kind of colloquialism for the original official designation, "licensed victualling house." In other words, pubs were originally intended to serve food to their patrons, with drink as a necessary accompaniment; now, of course, drink is what they chiefly deal in, although one may eat a light and often quite tasty meal in most of London's hundreds and hundreds of pubs.

What struck me most forcefully at first, I think, is that each pub I went into seemed to have a character of its own, depending in part, I suppose, upon the neighborhood; in part, upon the publican himself; in part, upon the kind of people who first started drinking there and so attracted others like themselves. Or—and this too I found most extraordinary—there might be two or even three different types of clientele in the same pub, for many pubs have a public bar, a saloon bar, and a lounge bar.

Although the visitor to London is constantly being told that the old class distinctions are fast disappearing, it seemed to me that the distinctions were fairly rigidly observed in many of the pubs I visited. Of course there are exceptions, and they are probably becoming more numerous all the time, but I did get the impression—especially outside central London—that blue-collar workers tended to gravitate to the public bar and those in white collars to the saloon bar. Each man himself, then, chooses his own class and this choice, it appears, is often made on the basis of family or social background.

In fact, the very existence of such distinctions seemed to me like a strange anachronism, as it would, I think, to anyone who came of age in the postwar Japanese world, where all titles (save imperial ones) were banished and where distinctions, however strict, are based on one's bank account and one's position in the business or professional world. Formerly, in Japan, the classes were more tightly controlled than anything England ever dreamed of, with feudal lords at the top and merchants at the bottom and farmers and artisans in between. It was a rare man indeed who succeeded in crossing the barriers between the classes. But with the entry of Japan into the modern world these barriers were soon overthrown, and now the Japanese merchant has come into his own.

I know it is foolhardy, and perhaps even presumptuous, for someone from a country as remote as Japan to talk about that nebulous but highly intricate institution known as the English class system—yet it is one of the things that interested me most, perhaps because it seemed to point up both the likenesses and the differences between Japan and England, between the country I came from and the country I was trying with all my heart to understand. Some knowledge of the English conception of "class" was, I felt, essential to any proper understanding. But it was so difficult! It was seldom discussed or explained: yet to me, it existed very clearly.

The likenesses between the two countries I found far easier to understand, for both are island kingdoms (rather pleased with their insularity) and both have at their heads constitutional monarchs who wield little or no real power. It has been pointed out that if the queen were presented with a bill calling for her execution, she would in theory be obliged to sign it; and the same, I suspect, would be true of our emperor who, since the Japanese defeat in 1945, has become "a symbol of the state."

Yet, despite the occasional agitation against the maintenance of the British royal house and (some say) its unnecessary expense, it is essential to the England that we now know. Without the monarch, there could hardly be a House of Lords; many people in fact advocate its abolition, but were it abolished then the entire character of

LONDON

British government would have to be changed. The same is hardly true of Japan. I think most Japanese, even the youth, have a genuine fondness for Tennō Heika, as we call the emperor, but the discarding of the throne would cause little change in the mechanism of the Japanese government or the daily life of the people.

On the other hand, the discarding of the British throne would involve first of all the abolition of the peerage—and that, as I say, would alter the country unrecognizably. The abolition of titles in postwar Japan and the substitution of councillors for peers in the National Diet were changes approved, it seems to me, by the majority of the Japanese people. Perhaps it would take a catastrophe proportionate to the Japanese defeat in 1945 to effect so tremendous a change in Britain. Although many of the young people I talked to expressed disdain for the monarchy and the peerage, I had the feeling that they would probably change as they took their places in the social hierarchy.

Certainly most of the older people I talked to in London seemed content to bask in the reflected glory of the great dukedoms and marquessates; they flocked in their thousands to see the stately homes thrown open, at a modest price, to the public; they believed (I think sincerely) that the Lords, however idle and disinterested some members might be, provides a workable system of checks and balances for the Commons. "Lords and Commons"—it is a unique system in our rough modern world, and I found it both fascinating and successful, wondering how I would like being a subject of the grandest monarch still reigning in the world. For the royal family itself living in this constitutional monarchy has its attractions. "We live in what virtually amounts to a museum," Prince Philip said a few years ago, "which does not happen to a lot of people."

London itself is, in its own way, a museum—a museum of many corridors ending in strange and surprising corners, where things are still being done as they have always been done and where things are being done as they have never been done before, where an ancient building and a new one live amiably side by side, where "flower children" invade Piccadilly Circus and "hippies" congregate on Parliament Hill.

This they were doing, when I was in London, every Sunday, and an American boy I met at an underground theatre invited me to join him at Parliament Hill on the following Sunday. He assured me I would not be sorry, and indeed I was not, although I found it quite a walk from the nearest subway station to the hill, which rises at the southern tip of Hampstead Heath. One of the rewards is the invigorating view over London from the summit.

This expedition was only the first of many that I made to Parliament Hill on succeeding Sundays, for there, on a specially built stage among the trees, were concerts of jazz and folk music, poetry readings, plays, and pantomimes. The audience is composed not of hippies alone but of older people from all over London who have come to enjoy the show and who pay no attention to the young lovers embracing beneath the trees. Children play nearby.

On the occasion of my first visit, a score of youths were devoting their energies and creative talents to the theme of the Buddha. Under the direction of two leaders, an American and a Filipino, there was a discussion, a brief play was performed, then there came the reading of poetry. Suddenly, most unexpectedly, a boy leading a horse passed through the audience: it was a "happening," and it was, as I came to learn on subsequent visits, a very typical one. My only complaint about Sundays on Parliament Hill was that the

19

happenings seemed to happen at impromptu hours: one afternoon I trekked up the hill to hear a rock concert, only to discover that it had taken place early that morning!

All this, of course, is predicated on the fact that the weather is being cooperative, and when it is—especially from the end of May through August—there are gatherings and concerts in almost all of London's parks and in many nonresidential squares as well. I suppose the most popular of all is the festival held twice yearly in Hyde Park, which may attract a hundred thousand or more young people: some sporting the "moddest" of "mod" clothes, others immodestly sporting no clothes at all; some listening intently to the music, others taking sun baths (providing the sun has decided to appear), still others locked in tight embraces.

And again, as always in London's parks, there are the older folk sitting quietly on benches, many with their pet dogs beside them. Coming from Tokyo, which is not famous for the number of its public parks, I think this was one of the things that impressed me most about London. In the summer always, within easy reach, there is a bit of earth, a tree-shaded bench, a garden blossoming.

We Japanese are famous gardeners, but we are inclined, I think, to consider a garden architecturally, which is why many of our famous so-called gardens are beds of fine white sand with carefully placed rocks. The British think otherwise; they all, young and old, rich and poor, enjoy the growing of flowers. The Chelsea Flower Show, for example, attracts people of all sorts, and as they wander about, they discuss the blooms with animation and absorption.

My newspaper friend, when he was in London, lived in a flat facing on a good-sized backyard. His next-door neighbor was constantly advising him on what seeds to buy and when to plant them and what particular fertilizer to use. One day, when I was visiting, the neighbor said to me: "What a joy it is to sit in a blossoming garden that you've brought to life! How satisfying to look at the plants and remember the difficulty you had rearing them! If you can't enjoy that, then you're not a true Londoner yet."

And one of my own neighbors, I learned, when she went off on a holiday, would carefully carry each of her many potted plants to a friend's house, to be cared for during her absence. When she returned, she would just as carefully carry the plants home again. This practice, probably common enough in London, struck me as one of the most remarkable things I had ever heard— probably because it is simply not, I think, an idea that would enter a Japanese head.

1-5. *London today*: Portobello Road shop (*overleaf*) specializing in the Union Jack; young folk (*above*) stroll through Hyde Park or along King's Road.

6-7. *Portobello Road Market* (*overleaf*): Saturday ▶
is the best day to go; and hunting for bargains,
obviously, is thirsty work.

25

9. *Selling records* in a lane behind Leicester Square, vendors seem more interested in each other than in prospective buyers.

8. *An unusual sight* is these young "sandwich girls" in Oxford Street; usually the boards are carried by older men.

10. *Hippies* hawk their own newspaper in Carnaby Street, once the heart of London's mod fashions, now a popular tourist sight.

11. *Girl* in Portobello Road Market offers for sale dresses she has made; a cardboard sign (here hidden behind the clothes) gives the prices.

12. *Kensington High Street* is a ▶ newer mecca for London's youth (*overleaf*).

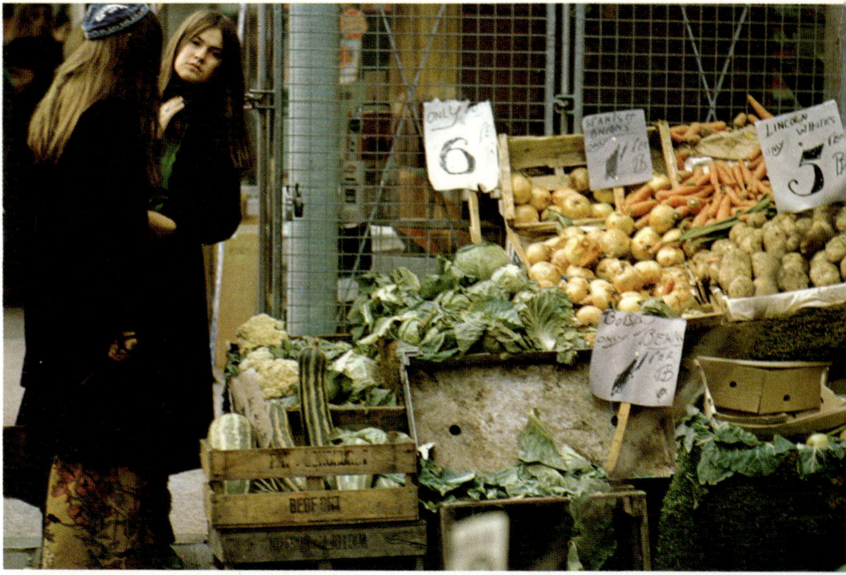
ONLY
6
LINCOLN
5

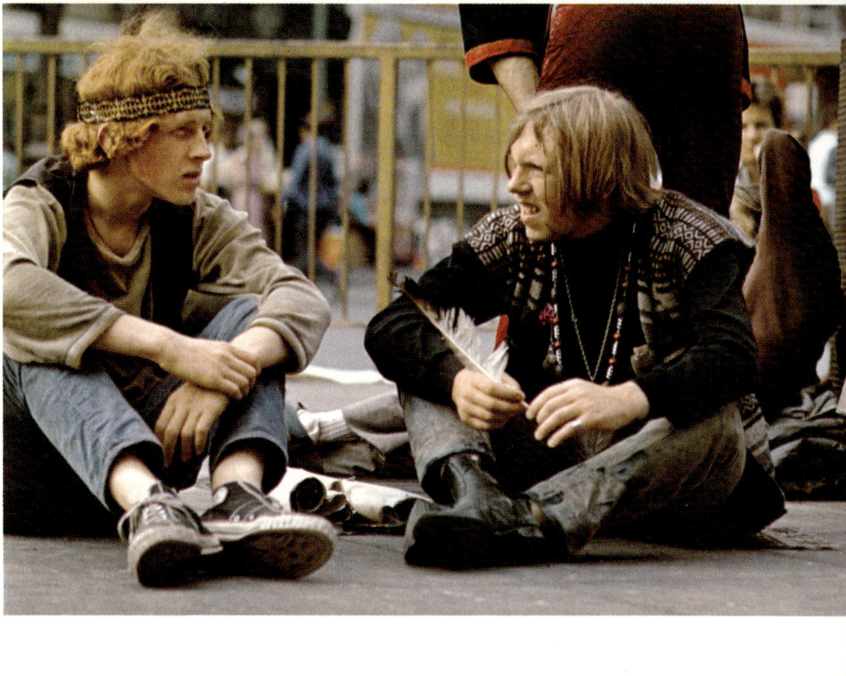

17. *Hyde Park* serves as the locale for a ▶
number of highly varied activities:
overleaf, a regimental reunion.

13-16. *London street scenes*: open-air food
stalls in Soho (*far left*); young people
in Piccadilly Circus (*lower left*); guitar
player in Portobello Road (*opposite*);
and *below* , another conversazione in
Piccadilly Circus.

22. *Another Hyde Park event* is an annual ▶ horse show (*overleaf*), held on the wide path near the Serpentine known as Rotten Row.

18-21. *Traditional London* is well represented by bowler-hatted businessmen in the City's streets (*left*) and by young Harrovians (*below left*) wearing their distinctive costume; *below right*, schoolboys and girls in Finsbury Park.

23-24. *Ascot races* (*see preceding page*) are England's most fashionable, where ladies (one of whom is shown above) deck themselves out in their finest.

25. *The Derby* (*right*) at Epsom: the victor is in the paddock after the end of the race. ▶

26-28. *Women of fashion* use Ascot Week as an excuse to let imaginations run riot. *Below left*, a woman reporter covering Ascot fashions; *center*, the enormous hat was designed by the lady herself; this suit today, tomorrow? (*below right*).

◄29. *Pop concert* (*overleaf*) at Compton Bay on the Isle of Wight, went on for five days and attracted some three hundred thousand young people.

48

30-33 *London's youth* is lured by rock concerts at Lewes and Hyde Park, and by a Hare Krishna meeting in Trafalgar Square (*second from right*).

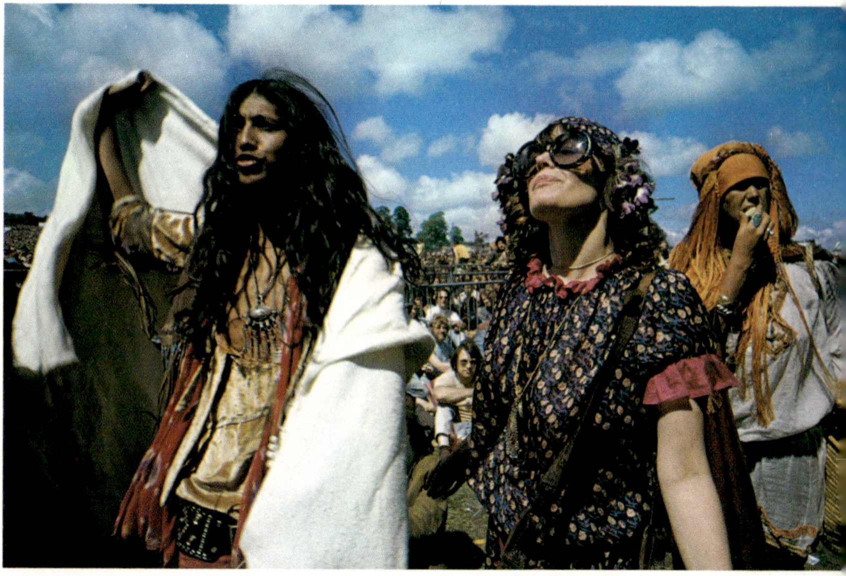

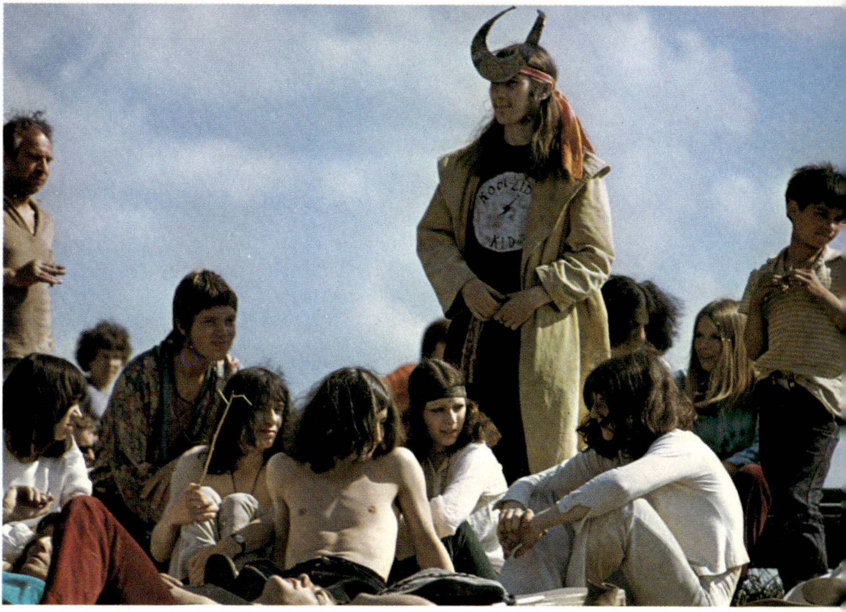

34-38. *Not only music* has its charms: colorful participants (*far left*) distract from the sound at a pop concert in Bath; Parliament Hill gatherings go in for music, poetry, pantomime, etc., (*lower far left*); Hell's Angels, carrying bicycle chains as weapons lurk menacingly on the fringes of a pop concert (*opposite*); one member of the audience at a Hyde Park concert (*below left*); and —charmed by the music (or is it the sun?)—some girls in Hyde Park show signs of ecstasy (*below right*).

39-40. *Further views (overleaf and page 94)*▶ of the "happening" on the Isle of Wight.

Present and Past

London's young people and its old! They seem so different in their approach to today's world, so thoroughly separated by that generation gap, and yet I had the feeling that binding them together was a quality uniquely theirs, a quality that perhaps they were unaware of themselves—and yet that they would not change for the world. It is as mysterious as the fact that the most radical of Tokyo students and the most staid of Tokyo's company presidents also share a quality that makes them—despite their deep divergences—Tokyoites and nothing else. And most of them would not want to be anything else.

The same is true of Londoners, and it may be true of London to an even greater extent than of Tokyo. I used to love to watch the youth cavorting in one of their favorite haunts and then go to a nearby park and exchange a word or two with some older woman sitting there in the sun—or more often the "nonsun." I once listened to a long-haired young man reading an ode to Victoria Station to a gathering of hippies; then, a little later, walking through Battersea Park, I encountered an old lady pushing a baby carriage. When I peeked inside, I saw—to my bewilderment—not a child at all but a little dog with glossy white fur. Beside the dog lay a bottle of milk. When I looked at the woman with some astonishment, she cried, "Her name is Lucy—isn't she beautiful?" Then, to the dog: "Lucy, look this way! The nice lady is going to take your picture."

In my country eccentricity, although it is not exactly prohibited, is not considered really good manners; in London, on the contrary, a person can do pretty much what he likes—so long, to be sure, as what he likes to do is not antisocial. He can live at his own pace, he can act as he pleases and say what he thinks—once again, so long as none of it is considered antisocial. At Speakers' Corner in Hyde Park near Marble Arch, where people congregate to listen to solvers of the world's problems, just about the only subjects that are taboo are how to put an end to the nation and how to assassinate the monarch.

Living pretty much as they choose, most Londoners grow old—or so it seemed to me—without the fear of loneliness that haunts so many Japanese as they embark upon their last years. And because Britain is a welfare state, there is not that terrible fear of old-age poverty either. I was amazed by the number of elderly men and women walking cheerfully and upright and quite alone on London's streets. Perhaps they were just taking a constitutional, perhaps they were on their way to do a bit of shopping, perhaps they were going to a park or a museum; in any case, they appeared to me, most of them, to be quite content with their lot and enjoying their remaining time on earth. I decided London would not be a bad place to spend one's declining years.

Nor is it a bad place, as the world has learned, to spend one's youth. The young, like the old, enjoy a freedom to express themselves that—to a visitor from a country like Japan—is positively astonishing. When I first came out of my self-constructed shell and started wandering about the city, I naturally enough took Piccadilly Circus as a kind of starting point. There, congregated around the statue of Eros in the center of the triangular square (if a square or a circus can be triangular!), were colorful bands of young folk— hippies and flower children and I hardly know what all.

Just as Eros is not Eros at all but rather the Angel of Christian Charity (built in the late nineteenth century in honor of the philan- thropic seventh Earl of Shaftesbury), and just as the Circus is neither round nor oval but rather triangular, so too did the young folk who flocked there contradict what I had begun to puzzle out about the rules of the British class system—for here, so far as I could make out, there was a total absence of class distinction. It seemed to make not a particle of difference whether one had not a penny in one's pocket and planned to spend the night in a sleeping bag in Hyde Park or whether one had a comfortable, perhaps even stately, home to go back to and had merely come to the Eros statue in order to be "with it." No one asked questions, no one listened for the "right" accent, no one cared how anyone else was dressed; everyone was free and equal, everyone was everyone else's friend. What they all wanted, these young people, was their freedom; I felt that if they could, they would take off and fly around the world like the wind.

To be sure, there were some who, the moment they spotted an obvious tourist, would stop their guitar-playing and singing and try to sell some rather indifferent paintings at outrageous prices, and there were others who would demand money to pose for photogra- phers; but after all, I reasoned, they would probably go hungry that night unless they got money from somewhere, and work was anathema. They were merely doing their thing, and if their thing included scrounging a few pennies in order to buy a bag or two of fried potatoes, well, I could not see that they were doing any harm—except perhaps to their own digestive systems!

The following year, with the coming of spring, I was surprised to see how few hippies and flower children now came to Piccadilly Circus, and those that did did not occupy the center of the square but instead remained in small groups outside the fence. I do not know whether the change came about because the metropolitan police department had decided to "rescue" London's most famous plaza or because its former denizens had simply decided to move somewhere else. Obviously, if I was to continue my curative process of learning to know the city, I would have to find out.

The answer was an obvious one: these free-as-the-wind folk were equally free in their shifting allegiance to one quarter or another. At one time it was Carnaby Street, where the miniskirt, among other "mod" clothes, is said to have originated, but after a time, as the tourists moved in, London's youth moved on.

One of the places they moved on to was the King's Road, Chelsea, once the center of a polite residential village but now well on the way to becoming as busy a shopping center as Bond Street or Knightsbridge. It still, however, remains a residential area, although chiefly for the rich, who inhabit the fashionable little streets between the King's Road and the Chelsea Embankment. As I wandered through this quarter one afternoon, I was struck by the fact that in London houses of a feather seem to flock together. You rarely see a grand house standing beside a shabby one; streets as well as squares have a distinctive character, which would suggest that in them live people of similar incomes and social status. I found this sort of homogeneity rather insipid when compared with the frantic variety of Tokyo. It is interesting to note, however, that celebrities as diverse as Thomas More, Nell Gwynn, and Oscar Wilde have all lived in Chelsea. For a time, after the end of the war, Chelsea became a haven for young artists, but now, with London prices soaring, the former studios are being remodelled into elegant homes for successful stockbrokers.

The King's Road itself begins at Sloane Square, a busy place, with small shops and a large department store, a theatre and a subway station, coffee houses and flower stalls; and it does not end until it reaches the River Thames. A stroll down its length can be very tiring—but also very invigorating, for there is great variety. And of course, as one strolls, one finds oneself obliged to stop from time to time for a cup of tea or something more substantial.

I was attracted to the Café Picasso, chiefly because its appearance reminded me somewhat of Paris cafés, although the cuisine did not strike me as particularly Gallic. But here, I discovered, was one of the meeting places for the King's Road tribe of young people as well as for models from a nearby agency who would drop in, in their glittering makeup, for a quick cup of tea between engagements.

It would be almost impossible, I should think, to list all the many pubs, the restaurants of so many various nationalities, and the glamorous boutiques for both women and men that line the length of the King's Road, although as one approaches nearer the Embankment, the road grows progressively less commercial. At the bottom is a fascinating warren of antique shops, where, after wandering around for an hour or so, one develops (I found) quite a thirst. The Red Lion is a pub to be recommended, and I frequently took visiting Japanese friends there.

Another place that my visitors (and I) enjoyed was the market in Kensington Church Street, not only because of the wealth of objects on display there—from old junk through antiques to ties a a yard wide—but also because of the wealth of strange, fantastically dressed young people, buyers and sellers both. It was a place of endless fascination for me, and as elsewhere in London where youth in all its variety and vitality congregated, it helped consolidate my joy at being alive and being there. I felt a bit like Shakespeare's Miranda, who, after her lonely island sojourn has ended, cries:

> How many goodly creatures are there here!
> How beauteous mankind is! O brave new world
> That has such people in 't!

Now I knew quite well that in my wanderings about London I had so far made little effort to visit its great, familiar sights, for to visit them meant—for me—to photograph them, and how could I do either with intelligence and originality without knowing at least a little about the history of this vast and ancient city? That, in turn, meant doing some homework, so with a sigh I got some books out of the library and settled down to work. It was a cold and wintry time of year, a time more conducive to reading than to wandering (and trying to read a light meter when there was hardly any light to read it by!); and fortunately I had by then almost completed the assignments that were paying for my London visit. I no longer felt any sense of anxiety on that subject.

To my great surprise I discovered, as I began to read, that there seem to be as many theories about the origin of the city as there are writers on the subject. I had somehow expected it to be as tidy as the origin of our ancient imperial capital of Kyoto, which was founded in the year 794 by Emperor Kanmu and completed, some ten years later, on a rectangular Chinese pattern. All very simple and straightforward—surprisingly so, perhaps, for Japan, which more often prefers ambiguity to directness. Now here were the English, who rather pride themselves on their ability to be explicit, without any sure knowledge of who first dwelt on the site of their capital, or when. I found this most un-English, and rather unsettling.

The increased knowledge that came as a result of the devastating German bombings during the war merely upset some previously held conceptions without substituting any hard new facts in their place. It used to be fairly generally accepted (or so I gathered) that what is now called the City was once a Celtic capital called Llyn-din, meaning "the lake fortress" (whence the Romans, when they came, derived the name Londinium). But postwar excavations have revealed no trace of that "Celtic capital," nor is there any historical evidence for its existence. About as far as most historians will go now is to grant that there was probably a small settlement there a few years before the coming of the Romans.

And even their arrival is not a firmly fixed fact. Once again there is a legend that has never been substantiated, for it used to be thought that Julius Caesar established a camp there in 55 B.C., but Caesar apparently crossed the Thames below London, and no mention of the "Celtic capital" is to be found in his writings. Some historians cling to the idea that there was a Roman settlement there before the first hard fact in London's history—the establishment of a camp on the site by troops of Emperor Claudius in A.D. 43.

What is now the City thus became both a Roman fort and port, and perhaps one of some importance, for a few years later Queen Boadicea took the trouble of invading and burning it. Soon thereafter London's famous Roman Wall was begun, which continued to protect London throughout the Middle Ages and of which small fragments still remain.

As in other colonies of Roman, there were temples and baths and comfortable villas in Roman London, but these began to disappear soon after the Romans were driven from Britain in the fifth century by Germanic tribes. Then there came Saxons and Danes, King Alfred and King Canute, and finally, in 1066, William the Conqueror, at which time, to a certain extent, the "modern" history of London begins.

Long before William, however, in fact as early as the seventh century, a small church was built on the hill where great St. Paul's now stands. As I strolled through the City, I begain by looking for traces of the Roman occupation but was soon, I must confess, beguiled away from my quest by the people I passed on the streets. Young men and old, they all wore dark suits and bowler hats and carried umbrellas even on sunny days: they were all, in one way or another, part of one of the world's most important financial centers. During the day the population of the City is half a million, but by nightfall it has dwindled to a mere five thousand; and the City is, I would guess, the only place in the world where a Christian church may be open six days a week—and closed on Sundays!

Once, not long ago, the City was paramount in the world's finances, but now of course it is rivalled or surpassed by Wall Street, and even Tokyo's Marunouchi district (which is modelled on it) now competes with it. The story goes that a Mitsubishi agent happened to be in London in 1872, wandering through the City and thinking what a splendid thing it would be for the new Japanese capital if it had a similarly concentrated financial center; not long after, he received word that Marunouchi had burnt to the ground and was being offered for sale by the government. He cabled his home office to buy it, which they did for the equivalent then of just over a million dollars. Today, of course, it is worth many hundred times that.

At first Marunouchi was modeled after the buildings of Lombard Street, the world's most famous banking and financial street, but with postwar reconstruction Tokyo's financial center, like London's, has taken on a more modern look. It could never, in any case, have rivaled the grandeur of the City, with the great Bank of England (founded in 1694), Mansion House (the eighteenth-century residence of the Lord Mayor), the Royal Exchange (first built in 1566-71), the Guildhall, the Inns of Court, and many, many other buildings of historical, artistic, or religious importance, including of course wonderful St. Paul's itself.

Before the Norman conquest in 1066, King Edward (called the Confessor because of his piety) built, on the site of earlier churches, the predecessor of what is now officially known as the Collegiate Church of St. Peter. Here Duke William was crowned king of England after he had conquered London, and here in a later construction virtually all of England's monarchs have been both crowned and buried—for the Collegiate Church of St. Peter is somewhat better known to the world as Westminster Abbey, so called because it stands to the west of the City.

The present church, an unrivaled example of Early English architecture, was begun in 1245 under King Henry III and was steadily embellished by succeeding monarchs. The west towers were not erected until the mid-eighteenth century, while the facade of the north transept was remodeled under Queen Victoria at the end of the nineteenth century. Thus, the fabric itself spans virtually the whole of English history since the Conquest, while the interior houses the remains not only of England's monarchs but also of many of her great men and women, scientists and field marshals, poets and musicians, statesmen and empire builders. There are also a number of monuments in the abbey to some of England's great who are buried elsewhere.

Most impressive, of course, are the Royal Chapels in the ambulatory, in particular that of Henry VII, a richly decorated structure dating from the early sixteenth century. The Chapel of Edward the Confessor stands on the foundation of the main apse of the church that he himself built, and in 1268 Henry III erected a handsome mosaic shrine to him in the new church. One of England's monarchs who is not buried in the abbey is the Conqueror himself, who died in Rouen in 1087 and was buried in Caen. His bones were not permitted to rest there, however, for in 1562 his tomb was pillaged by Huguenots.

Strangely, perhaps, it was this same William, bastard son of a daughter of a French tanner by a duke of Normandy, who gave London its charter (its bill of rights, so to speak) and these privileges of the city were reaffirmed in the Magna Carta. It was also William who began the building of the most fascinating structure in all London, the Tower; for, at the same time that he granted the city its charter, he was determined to impress upon its people the fact that he was in command. Accordingly, in 1078, he began the construction of what is now called the White Tower.

I kept no count of the number of visits I made to the Tower, so I cannot say with any accuracy how many times I got off the District line at Tower Hill, but I know that there was a fascination about it that called me back time and again. Partly it was the tremendous span of history embraced by the Tower, partly its varied architecture, partly the fact that among the many treasures it houses are the extraordinarily splendid crown jewels of England, and partly, no doubt, the dark doings that took place in the past in the numerous towers that comprise the Tower.

Here Queen Elizabeth I was herself imprisoned while she was princess, and here she ordered the execution of both Essex and Raleigh, although the latter was not in fact beheaded until after her death. Here Sir Thomas More, now a Catholic saint, was executed at the command of Elizabeth's father, Henry VIII, and here also Elizabeth's mother, Anne Boleyn, was beheaded on a charge of adultery so that Henry could take a third wife. I think probably a list of the people who have been either imprisoned or executed within the Tower would be almost as illustrious as a list of those who lie buried in Westminster Abbey. Certainly, between the two, the foreign visitor to London gains a most eloquent picture of the splendors and the tragedies of England's history.

To round out that picture, the visitor must of course pay a dutiful pilgrimage to Buckingham Palace, the London residence of the sovereign. Erected in the first years of the eighteenth century for the Duke of Buckingham, the building, then known as Buckingham House, was bought by King George III in 1761, but it was not until 1837, when Queen Victoria ascended to the throne, that Buckingham House became the permanent London home of the monarch. Meanwhile, it had been remodeled, under George IV and William IV, by John Nash; then in 1846 the east wing was added; and

LONDON

finally, in 1912 the facade that faces St. James's Park was built by Sir Aston Webb in only three months, during the absence of King George V and Queen Mary.

It is this façade that the visitor sees as he peers through the protective iron grillwork. When I first went there, I was astonished at how accessible to the public it seemed, remembering how our own emperor, when he is in Tokyo, resides within a palace well hidden from the world by wide moats and high trees. Actually, I learned later, the real façade fronts on the garden, which is not visible to the public except during summer garden parties to a certain number of invited guests. Webb's façade, although at first sight it seems very plain, is on close scrutiny very beautifully proportioned, and it is there, on a second floor balcony, that royalty appears on state occasions and there that the royal standard flies when the monarch is in residence.

In front of the palace stands the much-abused Victoria Memorial, looking (so its critics say) like a pastry chef's nightmare in white marble. Around the sitting figure of the queen cluster smaller statues representing the Victorian virtues—Truth, Motherhood, and Justice—as well as Science and Art, Naval and Military Power, Peace and Progress, Industry and Agriculture, and finally Victory accompanied by Courage and Constancy. How exotic all these great abstractions sounded to me! How unlike Japan, I thought, recalling the austere mausoleum of Emperor Meiji (Queen Victoria's contemporary) in Kyoto, and recalling also the fact that millions of Japanese have prayed at the Shinto shrine in Tokyo dedicated to Meiji. This is a distinction that even the great Victoria does not enjoy, for the English monarchs, although they have claimed the "divine right" of kings, have never been said to actually partake of divinity as was the claim of the Japanese emperors before defeat in 1945.

On the other hand, Tokyo has no official pageantry even remotely resembling that of London, of which the best-known example is, I suppose, the changing of the guard at Buckingham Palace. At first, I must confess, I could not understand why this ceremony should attract such enormous crowds, but as I came to know London and its people better and to know a bit more about the history of the country, I could see in the changing of the guard a logical expression of the relationship between the monarch and the country.

Exercising little real political power, perhaps none at all, the queen remains the symbol of Britain, and all the majestic royal pageantry is a symbol too—a symbol of stability and continuance of tradition, characteristics that (despite the tremendous changes that have overwhelmed Britain since the war) remain, I think, very dear to the English heart. The daily changing of the guard is but one manifestation of that basic love of tradition; so of course is the trooping of the colour on the queen's birthday; so is the annual procession of the lord mayor of London, when he rides in a state coach from the Guildhall to the Law Courts to take his oath of office; and so, par excellence, are such royal occasions as coronations and burials, when all the pomp of British tradition is given its fullest expression. I wonder at it, and I admire it; it constitutes an an island of stability in the turbulent postwar ocean.

The Duke of Buckingham's house was not, obviously, the first building to stand on so strategic a site as that now occupied by Buckingham Palace. What one can never forget, as one wanders

LONDON

about London, admiring its handsome eighteenth-century squares and streets and houses, is that they would probably not exist at all were it not for the Great Fire of 1666, a tragedy that destroyed a good part of the city. (It followed hard upon the Great Plague, during which it has been estimated that some hundred thousand Londoners died.)

Not many important buildings survived the Great Fire, although there were a few happy exceptions, among them Westminster Abbey and the Tower. An estimate made at the time says that eighty-nine parish churches and 13,200 houses were burnt to the ground; the material loss to the city has been put at around ten million pounds, although most historians agree that that is probably an understatement. All this occurred within four days, from the second to the sixth of September. I can think of nothing to equal it in the history of any other great city except for the incendiary bombings of Tokyo during the last war.

As with Tokyo, so with London: the city had to be rebuilt. The reconstruction of Tokyo began at once, spurred on by American aid and Japanese diligence; it is still going on, to be sure, as in all large cities throughout the world, but the main job of reconstruction was accomplished within a very short time. The rebuilding of London was undertaken almost at once, too, but proceeded, as was only to be expected, at a much slower pace; and it was not until the reign of Queen Anne in the early eighteenth century that the city began to take on a semblance of its present-day character. Both the Great Fire and the incendiary bombings were horrible catastrophes, but London was luckier than Tokyo, for the fire occurred at a time when the building of stately homes was still possible. The result is that London remains one of the most beautiful cities in the world—

a claim that not even the most devout Tokyoite would make for his postwar capital.

Much of London was, of course, destroyed during the Second World War too. German bombs took a terrible toll of both lives and property. Buckingham Palace did not escape, nor did Westminster Abbey, nor the Houses of Parliament, nor the Tower, nor St. Paul's Cathedral. More than half of London's houses were destroyed or damaged, but the present-day visitor to the city would find that terrible fact hard to believe. The great monuments have been restored and many of the fine eighteenth- and nineteenth-century squares returned to their former glory.

A decade after the Great Fire ended, Sir Christopher Wren began the construction of a new cathedral, for the old one had been entirely destroyed. The building, not wholly completed until 1710, is surely one of the most beautifully designed Renaissance-style churches in the world and one that occupies as secure a niche in English history as the Abbey itself. One of the deans of old St. Paul's was also one of England's very greatest writers, a poet of love lyrics whose sermons have never been surpassed. St. Paul's has a monument to John Donne as it has to many other of England's most illustrious sons; it is also the final resting place for many, including its own chief architect. On the wall above Wren's tomb is the inscription, *Lector, si monumentum requiris, circumspice*; freely translated, this means, "If you want a monument, look around."

Indeed, if the visitor to London requires a monument to Wren, he can find it in a hundred places by merely looking around, for Wren was the prime mover in the reconstruction that followed the Great Fire. He made designs for at least fifty churches that had been destroyed as well as for several important secular buildings. He also

laid out a town plan for the entire city, but practical considerations unfortunately prevented its being carried out.

London was fortunate in the architects that appeared after the Great Fire, for many were men of considerable talent, but she was most fortunate of all in Wren, surely one of England's greatest artists. Happily, his genius was recognized. King Charles gave him a free hand in the rebuilding of the cathedral and a knighthood as well. He was both president of the Royal Society and a member of parliament. Although, through political machination, he was dismissed from his post as royal surveyor of the works, Londoners to this day consider him their most honored architect. Throughout the war, I was told, during the worst of the German bombings, people looked to the dome of St. Paul's to make sure it was still there. So long as Paul's stood, London stood.

It was after my second winter in the English capital that I realized with something of a shock that I had actually completed every single commercial assignment I had undertaken to do. Once I mailed the last prints back to Japan, I would be free to go back there myself, but, what was far more exciting, I would also be completely free to explore London, although I was far from convinced that the pictures I would take would be worthy of my subject.

I estimated that I had enough money to last me another year, and I resolved to let nothing interfere with my project, for as I had come to know the city better, I realized how absolutely right old Dr. Johnson had been, even though he may, as was his wont, have exaggerated a trifle. Of course there is not in London *all* that life can afford (nor was there in the doctor's day either), but there was certainly more in London—I knew it now—than I could possibly absorb in the free year at my disposal. Remembering my first gloomy days there, I could no longer understand how I had permitted myself to approach so close to the edge of the abyss. I felt now that that strange neurotic girl could never have been me.

As winter had by then drawn to a close, I decided to celebrate my new freedom and the coming of a new spring with a boat ride up the Thames to Kew. I suppose it is a truism that all great old cities grew up along the bank or banks of a great river, and London is no exception. It is where it is because the Thames is there. Despite Dr. Johnson, no Londoner today would boast that the Thames passing through the city is to be compared with the Seine as it winds so handsomely through the center of Paris. Nevertheless, the view from Westminster Bridge (beneath which one boards the boat either downstream toward Greenwich or upstream to Richmond) is a splendid sight, and one that inspired Wordsworth to write his famous paean to London that begins: "Earth has not anything to show more fair. . . ."

As one heads up toward Kew, one passes a number of famous buildings, the Houses of Parliament on one side, Lambeth Palace on the other, then the Tate Gallery and Chelsea, but I found myself more interested in the domestic scenes at Fulham and Hammersmith, with lines of freshly done laundry hanging in the yards of small houses and blocks of flats where working people live. Now and then I could hear the crow of a cock. I think perhaps it was coming upon these scenes of domestic, working class tranquility so unexpectedly that I found especially moving.

From Putney on, the eye is constantly delighted by the graceful white swans of the Thames—though some, alas, have been dyed gray by the oil that has contaminated the river. I had always been under the impression that all the swans in England belonged to the monarch, but now I discovered that the queen shares them with two city companies—the Vintners and the Dyers. For a moment I felt a deep surge of nostalgia as I recalled the swans, white and black both, that inhabit the moats surrounding Tokyo's imperial palace.

Kew's Royal Botanical Gardens were established in 1759 by Princess Augusta (mother of King George III), came into the possession of the state during the reign of Queen Victoria, and now constitute one of the most beautiful sights in the vicinity of London and one of the most important botanical collections in the world. There are, I was told, over forty thousand different kinds of living plants in the gardens! Even in the depth of winter, when snow lies thick upon the ground, tropical plants luxuriate in great glasshouses.

I spent a very happy day at Kew, and as spring wore on and became summer I returned quite often; as well as exploring some of London's many other parks and gardens: Regents Park, St. James's Park, Holland Park, and of course Kensington Gardens and Hyde Park, to list but a few of them. Each, it seemed to me, had a character of its own, a unique attraction.

Hyde Park, to be sure, is the most famous and also (I would suppose) the most frequented. It is still officially the property of the Crown and has been since 1536, when Henry VIII sequestered it for himself from among the possessions of Westminster Abbey. He kept it as his own private hunting ground, as did his daughter Elizabeth, but some years later Charles I opened it to the public. Hyde Park's famous Ring, for many years one of the centers of London fashion, was altered and enlarged in the 1730's when Queen Caroline ordered the construction of the Serpentine. Not the least of the park's attractions is Speakers' Corner, at the top end, beside the Marble Arch. I happily spent hours there, listening and looking.

In fact, as I wandered through Hyde Park, in good weather and bad, admiring the long stretches of trees and flowers, the lawns, the waterfowl in the Serpentine, the relaxed faces of Londoners blessed with this broad green haven in the midst of their busy city, I kept wishing that Mitsubishi's agent had been strolling there instead of in the City when he heard that burnt-out Marunouchi was for sale. The possession of such a treasure as Hyde Park might persuade even frenzied Tokyoites that the search for money is not life's only charm.

Again and again, as I began reluctantly to accept the fact that my London sojourn was drawing to its inevitable end, I found myself overcome by the sheer variety of the city's attractions. There is something in London for everyone, no matter what his tastes may be, from the National Gallery to a Soho striptease, a gambling club, or a cricket match.

A glance at the morning newspaper tells the visitor what major plays, concerts, operas, ballets are being performed, but there are also the so-called underground theatres, which are usually not listed in the newspapers but which are well worth investigating. I particularly enjoyed going to a place called the Round House, in Chalk Farm Road, where there are not only small theatres but also pubs and snack bars mainly frequented by young people. One could not only see some far-out play or movie but afterwards find oneself discussing it with others, for here I encountered none of the frigidity I had been warned was typical of the British character. Here everyone (at least everyone under thirty) was acceptable and

LONDON

accepted. Then, too, I went often to the National Film Theatre, which showed revivals of old and foreign movies.

Now that I am back in Japan, I find it hard to believe that a city which is actually smaller than Tokyo offers so much more to see and to do. One could easily spend weeks at the National Gallery and the British Museum alone, not to mention such other great collections as the Tate, the Victoria and Albert, and the Wallace. Smaller galleries, but also first rate, are those of Dulwich College and the Courtauld Institute; and there are the two displays of objects from the incredibly rich royal collection—that at Hampton Court and the ever-changing exhibition in the South Wing of Buckingham Palace, where one pays one's entrance fee to a footman in royal livery.

Then there are the great houses that have been opened to the public, the palaces, and the old City churches—and as sightseeing tends to be dry work, the sightseer will often find himself (or herself) seeking sustenance at the nearest pub or perhaps journeying to a further favorite. One pub that I always enjoyed is Dirty Dick's, opposite Liverpool Street Station. The pub has not, so the story goes, been cleaned once in its two and a half centuries of existence; and it is a story I believe, for soot seemed to hang like icicles from the ceiling. I kept wondering, somewhat uneasily, when one of those "icicles" was going to drop into my drink, but none ever did, and I found the atmosphere of the pub much to my liking, for everyone was friendly and talkative—and the smoked salmon was superb.

Wandering about the city, often in the rain, toting my camera and guidebook, I found that my thirst did not always coincide with the opening hours of the pubs, and then I had to make do with what the English call a nice cup of tea. At first I did not think it was nice at all. We Japanese are accustomed to green tea, drunk straight, and the idea of black tea with milk and sugar did not attract me. And I decided that the British must be a very lazy people, since they did not even bother to heat the milk before pouring that strong black brew into it. In the course of time, however, I grew accustomed to those nice cups of tea and eventually even learned to like them. I would find myself dropping into a tearoom to plan my excursion for the day, and then a little later dropping into another because the pictures did not seem to be going right or because it looked like rain or because. . . . Well, like the British, I discovered that reasons for drinking a nice cup of tea are endless. I discovered also (making cups of tea in my room) that hot milk is definitely counterproductive when it comes to improving the flavor of the tea.

41. *Sentries*, looking like lead soldiers, still guard the entrances to many of London's oldest and most important monuments.

42-44. *Beside Westminster Bridge* rises the splendid thirteenth-century fabric of Westminster Abbey (*far left*); and beside that stand the Houses of Parliament (*opposite and below*), built in the mid-nineteenth century on the site of the Palace of Westminster, once the residence of the monarch.

45. *The Tower of London*, where so many Englishmen met their death, now houses barracks, museums, the Crown Jewels, beefeaters, tourists galore, and a licensed restaurant.

46. *Tower Bridge*, built at the end of ▶ the nineteenth century, has twin drawbridges, which can be lifted for the passage of large vessels but which are now used only once or twice a day.

49. *Pigeons*, pedestrians, and public ▶ speakers vie for elbow room in Trafalgar Square; the National Gallery is in the background.

47. *Beefeaters*, officially known as Yeoman Warders, guide tourists through the maze of towers and other buildings that make up the Tower.

50. *Piccadilly Circus*, taken over for a time by hippies and flower people, has now been restored by the authorities to ordinary citizens. (*below right*). ▲

48. *St. Paul's Cathedral* (seen here from Fleet Street) was built by Sir Christopher Wren after the Great Fire had destroyed its ancient predecessor.

PAN AM

PICCADILLY THEATRE
MAN OF LA MANCHA
Coke
GUINNESS TIME

51-53. *Among the sights of London*: a small theatre (*far left*) where the audiences are mainly youthful; the familiar double-decker bus (*opposite*), which has become a trademark of the city; (*below*) young people and Chelsea pensioners often go shopping, or window-shopping, in the King's Road.

54. *Dirty Dick's,* one of London's many hundreds of pubs, claims it has never been cleaned since it was founded two and a half centuries ago.

55. *For every pub* there is a pub sign, many of them landmarks like this one at Harrow on the Hill (home of Harrow School) ten miles from the center of London.

58. *Military band* (*overleaf*) accompanies ▶
the colorful changing of the guard at
Buckingham Palace.

56-57. *Club and pub*: the bunny club
(*opposite*) is open twenty-four hours a
day for members only; the public house
(*below*) observes fixed licensing hours.

59-60. *Folk dancing* is still alive and well: *preceding page*, Britain's ancient morris dance; *above*, a Scottish dance at an outdoor fete in Chelsea.

94

Revelry and Rest

I often dropped into Harrod's to have my cup of tea and in fact found their self-service snack bar a very pleasant place for lunch. I preferred Harrod's to the other department stores, although I was of course much impressed by the grandeur of Fortnum and Mason and by the good quality and modest prices of Marks and Spencer. Not being able to afford London's great restaurants, I was not unduly impressed by the ones I could afford, so when I did not cook my own meals or eat with friends I used to go either to snack bars like that at Harrod's or else to one of London's many Chinese restaurants. Two that I particularly liked were in Soho, both modestly priced and both serving superb Chinese food.

In any case I always enjoyed wandering around Soho and gladly seized on every excuse to go there. Lying to the north of Piccadilly Circus, Soho is a strange mixture of good restaurants and bad, cheap drinking clubs and striptease shows, prostitutes and junkies, and ordinary Continental-style grocery shops where the most respectable housewives go to find foods that are not readily available elsewhere in London. Soho is pierced by Shaftesbury Avenue, which, as it has many theatres on it, has become a synonym for London's theatre district just as Broadway has for New York's.

LONDON 🚌

Although Soho could not possibly be anywhere but London, it has a distinctly foreign flavor to it, and that (they say) is the result of an influx of French Huguenots after the Revocation of the Edict of Nantes in 1685. Ever since, Soho has been a refuge for foreigners of all nationalities. As to how it acquired its peculiar name, no one seems to be altogether sure, although one story has it that "So-hoe!" was the call to arms of the Duke of Monmouth (who had earlier lived in the district) when he tried to foment a rebellion against his uncle, King James II. The rebellion failed, Monmouth (who was a bastard of Charles II) was executed, and Soho (if the story is true) got its name.

If the story is not true, it should be, for Soho is still associated in the minds of most Londoners with violence of one kind or another—fist-fights and robberies and even murder. Theoretically, prostitutes no longer patrol its streets, but they are very much in evidence, soliciting from the upper windows of the old-fashioned houses that characterize most of Soho.

Sex is as much a part of the Soho scene as foreign food, and everywhere one sees movie houses featuring nude films, advertisements for striptease shows, and raffish pubs. Men, so I was told, are frequently importuned by ponces offering either girls or blue films or both. Such entertainment (they say) is likely to be quite expensive and not without its element of danger.

I was assured that it would be quite all right for me to go to one of the better striptease shows, and I was amazed to see a large number of women in the audience. Somehow I had expected it would be almost entirely composed of men, but once the show started I could understand why it attracted people of both sexes, for many of the dancers were excellent, the stage settings were quite handsome, and the show went on uninterruptedly for two hours. During this time, of course, one could order drinks.

Popular also in Soho are dance halls, in most of which the rock music is so loud I should imagine anyone who frequents them regularly is in danger of suffering permanent ear damage. Most of the patrons, it seemed to me, were young people—which was not true of Soho's gambling clubs. Of course there are gambling clubs all over London now, and the best are in more exclusive neighborhoods, but these are also difficult to join, particularly for a not very well-heeled working girl, whereas with many of the Soho clubs one may become an instant member simply by showing one's passport. Also, of course, one may buy chips of fairly small denomination. The favorite games, so for as I could see, were blackjack and roulette.

An unusual aspect of London night life is its pubs that feature drag shows. One that I particularly enjoyed was close to Vauxhall Station (a five-minute bus ride from Victoria Station). It seemed to me to be as crowded every night as a Tokyo subway during rush hours, and the reason was easy to see: for the price of a pint or half-pint of beer patrons of the pub may enjoy a lively show where men dressed elaborately as women kick up their heels on a small stage. Most of the customers seemed to be blue-collar workers who objected strenuously, and in fairly strong language, when at the end of the evening closing-time was announced. The vivid arguments between the management and the drinkers contributed greatly to my knowledge of contemporary English.

It would obviously be impolite not to say a word or two about London sporting life, for was not the battle of Waterloo won on the playing fields of Eton? Anyway, from time to time the sporting life of London became a part of my own personal life, for the stop nearest to my house on the Piccadilly subway line was Finsbury Park, and the stop before that was Arsenal, a rather dismal and gloomy station most of the time but some days full of a jostling, shouting, milling throng. Those were the days when there were soccer games at Highbury Stadium (the home of Arsenal, one of England's most famous soccer clubs).

Soccer is officially known, I believe, as association football, as distinct from a game called rugby football. It is England's most popular sport and when there was a game at Highbury Stadium the entire neighborhood knew about it. Not only would the station itself be crowded with young men and old wearing brightly colored mufflers and shouting at the tops of their voices, but all the neighborhood pubs would also be jammed.

Even Piccadilly Circus might be invaded by victorious fans after a game, and the statue of Eros would be fenced in for protection. On occasion I saw mammoth snake dances in celebration that the resigned police did not even try to prevent. So popular is the game in Britain that there are, I was told, over thirty thousand soccer clubs with three-quarters of a million players. The most important game of the year is the Cup Final at Wembley at the beginning of May.

And then of course there is cricket, which is even more confusing than association football. There must be something peculiarly British about it, as it is played, I believe, only in Britain or in places where British influence has been predominant. My own country has taken to baseball and bowling with alacrity, as well as to soccer, but I do not know of any Japanese cricket players. I did go to St. John's

Wood to see Lord's cricket ground, headquarters of the Marylebone Cricket Club and England's most important cricket ground. Here games are played from May until September, with the university and public school matches in July.

At the end of June the talk is all about Wimbledon, where world championship tennis matches are held over a period of two weeks. For the record, the ground belongs officially to a body known as the All England Lawn Tennis & Croquet Club. All over London, department stores start selling parasols as early as May with the catch phrase: "Buy one for Wimbledon."

Around the same time of year (the end of May and mid-June) come the great horse races. The first, at Epsom, was established by the Earl of Derby (whence its name) in 1780 and always takes place on a Wednesday at the end of May or the beginning of June. Derby Day, with its great and varied crowds, is indeed a fascinating sight, even for someone who is not greatly interested in the racing of horses, for in addition to the eager spectators are itinerants, many of them gypsies, who have come to the track days before the races in order to construct a gigantic amusement center, with merry-go-rounds, shooting galleries, and all the usual "attractions" of a fun fair.

For me as a woman the paramount racing spectacle of the year is Ascot Week, which dates from 1711 and is usually held two weeks after Derby Day. Here no gypsies come but rather the highest of London society, for Ascot has become famous as a place for ladies of fashion to exhibit their most splendid frocks. On the Thursday of Ascot Week, Gold Cup day, the Queen drives up in state; and around the entrance to the Royal Box, the entire five days of the races, cluster reporters, photographers, and unabashed gapers.

LONDON

Now and then friends or friends of friends from Japan would look me up, and then of course I would be expected to show them around a bit. I generally refrained from taking them to the obvious places, for after all anyone can find his way to Westminster Abbey or Buckingham Palace, but rather preferred to take them to places they might miss on their own.

For instance, I would take them on one of my favorite late afternoon walks, beginning in Trafalgar Square at the foot of Nelson's column, amid the constant flutter of pigeons and people. From there we would walk to neighboring Charing Cross Station, then cross the Thames by way of the footbridge and continue on to the Royal Festival Hall, built beside the river on the South Bank for the 1951 Festival of Britain Exhibition. There, in the Festival Hall tea room, I would introduce my Japanese friends to the sacred rites of a nice cup of British tea, and to the splendid view if we were lucky enough to get seats near one of the windows.

In any case, once we had drunk our tea and eaten some pastries, we would go for a short walk along this part of the South Bank, admiring the Abbey and the Houses of Parliament across the water. Then, as the sun began to set, we would cross back to the other side by way of Westminster Bridge, listening to the chimes of Big Ben and watching the Houses of Parliament merge into the evening sky. Then we would wander slowly back along the Victoria Embankment to Charing Cross Station, having enjoyed a pleasant hour's walk amid the magic of London.

Or I might take my visiting friends to one or another of my two favorite markets—Portobello Road or Petticoat Lane. The former is a five-minute walk from Notting Hill station and is at its liveliest on Saturday mornings. There is a food market as well as a section devoted to new clothing, but it is chiefly the old clothing, the junk, and the genuine antiques that are the great lure. Portobello Road market is familiar to all Londoners, many of whom come to enjoy the commontion if not to buy, but I had a feeling my Japanese friends might find it a bit overpowering if they went on their own.

For it is indeed a raucous and sometimes a bewildering experience: with hippies wandering along the crowded road, playing their guitars and begging for money; with Hell's Angels all in black leather, sporting their tattoos and also canvassing for money; with Hare Krishna zealots dancing among their disciples; with people waiting impatiently for the pub in the central part of the road to open; and with the eccentric shopkeepers loudly hawking their wares.

Of these, two seem to be particularly famous. One is a huge man strikingly tattooed wherever the naked skin is visible; one can hardly help wondering about the rest of him! Although tattooing is said to have been introduced to the West by sailors who encountered it in Far Eastern ports, I have never seen anything in Japan to compare with the decorations sported by this Portobello Road shopkeeper. The other is a woman, the owner of a shop that specializes in lead figures of British soldiers and in objects, from umbrellas to curtains, made out of the British flag. The woman herself always wears a dress which is also composed of bits of the Union Jack. Sometimes, I noticed on various trips, a young man who worked in the shop would deck himself up in a red uniform with a Union Jack tie.

Prices of the junk at Portobello Road, as well as of the real antiques, are not particularly cheap. Haggling, which of course would be unthinkable in a good London shop, is the order of the day here, but as the original asking prices are high one seldom comes away with a bargain. However, the show itself is worth paying a little bit extra for.

The other market that I liked to visit, but for quite different reasons, was located in that section of London called the East End, associated for centuries with the poor, with slums and docks and teeming street life. The market at Petticoat Lane has no vast assortment of old junk, like that in Portobello Road, but rather confines itself to supplying the average citizen's daily needs—food, kitchenware, bed linen, blankets, and the like. Sunday morning is the time to go: the market usually folds up its tents around one-thirty in the afternoon.

Everywhere are hoarse-voiced hawkers describing the goods they are offering in the most glowing terms. I noticed, if I stood long enough in front of one of the hawkers, the initial price asked would descend with increasing sharpness. It also seemed to me that some of the hawkers had a shill or two in the crowd and some had men hired to boo them (although my English friends always assured me that these were ordinary bystanders), perhaps to increase the crowd's interest or sympathy.

Another feature of Petticoat Lane on a Sunday morning is a vast number of small stalls selling hamburgers, sausages, fried scallops, boiled shrimps, and jellied eels. I found British sausages to be a rather slowly acquired taste, but the eels I took to at once. They are not all that different from our Japanese eels, but the British like to pour a great deal of vinegar over them, which I found to be quite a good idea. Thrown in, free of charge, is all the French bread you can eat.

REVELRY AND REST

Although I have by nature a taste for slums, I found the East End itself a disappointment. Walking along the dilapidated streets that continue to exist (many are being renovated in London County Council housing developments), I detected little of the strong "smell of life" that I associate with slum areas. Most of the people I passed seemed to be old, to have given up the struggle; at the same time, I saw very few children playing in the streets—probably because families with small children are given preference in the new developments and because even in the East End there are many green squares as well as the 217 acres of Victoria Park.

One popular area that was anything but a disappointment to me was Trafalgar Square, to which I would frequently find my feet taking me without my head having given any conscious instructions to that effect. I like everything about the square: the great column erected to commemorate Admiral Nelson's victory at Trafalgar, the splendid fountains, the ubiquitous pigeons, the crowds, the noble entrance to the National Gallery, the fact that this is—despite its associations with empire and royalty—very much a people's square.

Here, mostly on Saturday and Sunday afternoons, vast throngs congregate at open-air meetings, listening to speakers extol one form of government over another or one kind of trade union or one brand of religion. During the last month of the year, a huge Christmas tree is set up in the square, and on the last night of the month the square is packed with people seeing the old year out and the new one in.

Although very few Japanese are Christians, they have adopted Christmas almost as a national holiday, but the role of Christmas, like that of New Year's, is the opposite in Japan from what it is in

103

the West. In the West, Christmas is almost always a family celebration, while in Japan Christmas Eve is an excuse for an outburst of wild drinking. Then, in the West, people often celebrate New Year's Eve publicly, while in Japan it is very much a private festival based on Buddhist and Confucian precepts and originally celebrated according to the Chinese lunar calendar.

New Year's Eve in Trafalgar Square, thus, was something of a shock to me—but a very pleasant one. The square is jammed with people, young and old, and although the temperature may be well below freezing point, exuberant youths leap into the two fountains. Then comes the sound of Big Ben announcing that midnight has arrived. Everyone shouts "Happy New Year!" and kisses whomever he pleases. Young girls even kiss the bobbies standing around the square to be sure that nothing gets out of hand. And someone begins to sing "Auld Lang Syne. . . ."

It is with the haunting memory of that bittersweet song that I would like to close this story of my stay in a city that has meant more to me than I can possibly say in words. Perhaps my pictures tell a better story.

Southeast England

61-63. *Public parks*—large and varied—are one of the most attractive features of London life. Green Park (*preceding page and opposite*), although it lies in the center of London is a haven of quiet, natural beauty. Victoria Park (*below*) provides playing space for those who dwell in the city's overcrowded East End.

64-67. *Speakers' Corner,* at the top end of Hyde Park, is one of the chief places where Londoners with something preying on their minds may give it air. Almost anything goes. Those who have wearied of being harangued may slip into the park and have a cup of tea beside the Serpentine.

68-69. *Children* are well provided for: *left*, the London Zoo; *above*, a fun fair at Battersea Park.

70. *Sundays*, weather permitting, painters as yet unknown exhibit their works beside Green Park. ▶

71-76. *Virtually* every London park has an area specially reserved for children. Shown here are scenes from Kensington Gardens, Regent's Park, and Crouch Hill (in a northern district of the city).

77. *Crouch Hill*, like many outlying districts,
provides wide fields which are places of refuge
for children who want to escape from traffic.

78. *Kensington Gardens,* just beside Hyde Park,
are frequented by children with their mothers
or nursemaids; *above,* beside the Round Pond.

79-82. *Older folk* are well looked after too in the new London: *opposite*, a housing development in the slummy East End; *below left*, listening rather skeptically to an orator at Speakers' Corner; *below right*, taking the dog for a constitutional on the outskirts of the city; and *far right*, having a good gossip on a bench in the King's Road.

83. *Lucy*, wheeled out to see the world by her best
friend, poses languidly for her photograph.